The Most

by Jan Jones

![Harcourt]

Orlando   Boston   Dallas   Chicago   San Diego

Visit *The Learning Site!*

www.harcourtschool.com

Some people can name the tallest building in the world. Some people know the name of the longest river. In this book, you will learn about five living things that are special in some way.

The Tallest: Redwood Trees

Redwood trees are the tallest trees on Earth. They can grow as tall as a building with thirty floors. Their bark can be a foot thick. If you held hands with twenty other children to form a circle, you might fit around a redwood tree. These trees can live to be 2,000 years old!

Redwood trees do not have deep roots. Instead, the roots spread out around the base of the tree. The roots of several trees join together. This helps them stand when strong winds blow.

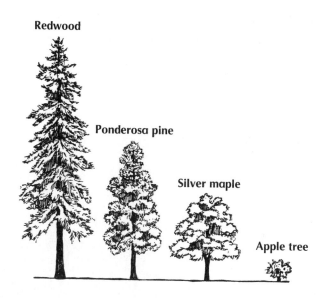

Redwood

Ponderosa pine

Silver maple

Apple tree

As a redwood tree grows, its lower branches do not get much sun. The leaves cannot make food without enough sunlight. The lower branches die.

The leaves on the higher branches keep the tree alive. The highest branches cannot get water from the roots. The roots are too far away. They must get water from the air. The air in their habitat is moist. The trees pull water from the air through their spiny leaves. The water in the air is like nectar to these thirsty trees.

A redwood tree grows from seeds, like other trees. A redwood tree can also grow other ways.

A very strong wind can topple a redwood. The top of the tree snaps off. A new tree can grow from the stump that is left in the ground. In fact, a ring of trees can grow from the stump of a fallen tree. New sprouts also grow as the fallen tree decomposes.

Some trees living today could be from the stumps of trees that lived 20,000 years ago!

In the time of dinosaurs, redwood trees grew in many parts of the world. Now they live along the west coast of the United States. In many places the trees are protected by law.

New redwoods grow from a stump.

Anaconda 20 ft.

Rattlesnake 4 ft.

Garter snake 2 ft.

The Longest: Anacondas

The longest snake in the world is the anaconda. An anaconda can be 20 feet long. That's about as long as you and four or five of your friends lying head to toe. This snake can weigh 235 pounds. That means an anaconda can weigh about as much as four or five of you, too.

Anacondas belong to the same snake family as pythons and boas. They live in rain forests in South America. They live near rivers.

Anacondas eat birds, crocodiles, small mammals, and other snakes. These snakes have very powerful muscles. They wrap their bodies around each animal they catch. They squeeze the animal until it dies.

5

An anaconda's jaw is not connected at the back. It can stretch its mouth wide enough to swallow a big animal. It eats the animal whole. Then the snake rests for a few days. An anaconda does not eat very often.

On land, anacondas travel through the brush to hunt. They climb trees. They wait on a branch and watch for their next meal to walk by.

In the water, anacondas stay just beneath the surface. There, they wait for their next meal to swim by.

When an anaconda is in danger, it tries to get away. If it can't get away, it will fight. If an anaconda is trapped, it will bite. This snake has teeth. Those teeth can make deep, painful cuts. However, its venom is not as dangerous as the venom from a rattlesnake.

Some people have killed anacondas for their beautiful skins. They have green skins with black marks.

It is against the law to capture anacondas. Can you imagine having one as a pet? That is a very bad idea.

The Fastest: Cheetahs

Cheetahs are the fastest of all the cats in the world. They have very strong legs. Their tails help them make quick turns. Their claws grab the ground as they run. Their hind legs push with powerful force. Their long bodies fly over the ground. These cats can run up to seventy-one miles an hour. The fastest human runners can go only about thirteen miles an hour.

Cheetahs do not roar like other big cats. They bark like dogs. Sometimes they chirp like birds. A cheetah's chirp can be heard a mile away! Just like other cats, cheetahs purr. When they are in danger, they make noises that sound like meows.

Cheetahs live on the grasslands and plains of Africa. They eat meat. They hunt twice a day—in the early morning and late afternoon. Cheetahs perch on a tree branch. They wait for a herd of antelope or other animals to come near.

When a herd passes by, the cheetah finds a weak or young animal. The big cat follows that animal. It will get very close before it attacks. Then it will spring with a burst of speed. The cheetah uses its strong jaws to pull the animal down.

Male cheetahs hunt together in small groups. Females hunt alone. They hunt to feed themselves and their cubs. The cubs have spotted coats. They also have long, gray hair on their heads and backs. When they are very little, the mother has to leave them alone while she hunts. The long gray hair helps hide the cubs.

Once the plains were teeming with antelope. There are not as many now, so cheetahs have less to eat. Cheetahs have also been hunted by people for their beautiful fur. There are fewer cheetahs than ever before. Today there are fewer than fifteen thousand left.

The pygmy shrew is only half as long as a field mouse.

The Smallest: Pygmy Shrew

The pygmy shrew is the smallest mammal in North America. An adult weighs less than a dime. Its body is less than 3 inches long.

These little creatures live in woods and wet, grassy places. They spend most of their time underground. They raise their little babies in the soft, dark nests they dig. The babies are as small as your fingernail.

Pygmy shrews will attack any animal that they think is an enemy. The shrews don't seem to know how very small they are. They may be little, but they are very brave.

Pygmy shrews live in several areas of the United States. They live in the Great Lakes region and in some parts of New England. These creatures also live in the southern Appalachian Mountains. Some live in parts of Colorado.

Pygmy shrews are very active. They run back and forth above the ground. Below the ground, they use a lot of energy digging tunnels. They move about in the day as well as the night.

These tiny animals need lots of food. They need to eat about every three hours. They eat insect eggs. They also eat small worms, spiders, and beetles.

Every day, pygmy shrews eat about twice their own weight in food. If you did that, you might eat almost a hundred pounds of food a day.

Like other mammals, pygmy shrews are covered with hair. A mother shrew gives birth to three to eight babies every year.

When they are under the ground, pygmy shrews are safe. When they are above ground, they are in great danger. They have many enemies. Hawks and snakes hunt the shrews. Pygmy shrews have glands that give off a bad smell. Sometimes they are killed but not eaten. Their bad smell may be the reason. Their smell may also tell the animals hunting them where they are.

The Strangest: Platypuses

You might think that this photo was made by cutting and pasting together pictures of different animals. It was not. This strange animal is real! It is a platypus.

This animal has a bill and webbed feet like a duck. It has claws and fur like a cat. It has a flat tail like a beaver. Like a bird, it has ears that cannot be seen. Platypuses live only in eastern Australia. They weigh about five pounds. They are sometimes called "duckbills" because they look as if they have a duck's bill.

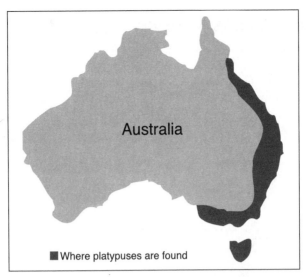

This map shows the areas in Australia where platypuses are found.

Platypuses live in tunnels that they dig along the banks of rivers. They are great swimmers. They can stay underwater for two minutes or longer.

Under the water, platypuses use their snouts to scoop up worms and other creatures from the river bottom. They feed at night. By morning, they may have eaten five pounds of food.

Their bodies tend to float. To stay under the water, platypuses have to keep swimming downward. They use their webbed front feet as paddles. Their hind feet help them steer. They keep their eyes closed under the water. Their special bills help them search out food in the muddy bottom.

Platypuses store food in pouches inside their cheeks. Instead of teeth, adults have plates in their mouths that they use to chew food.

Like other mammals, platypuses have hair. Like birds and reptiles, females lay eggs. A female platypus makes a nest in a tunnel. She lays two to four eggs. She uses her flat tail to hold the eggs against her belly for about two weeks. When the babies hatch, they have no fur. The mother feeds the babies with her milk.

Now you know a little about the tallest, longest, fastest, smallest, and strangest living things. Read more about them on your next visit to the library!